Coloring ART

Illustrated by

SK SAMARRA KHAJA

Photo by Ann Price

Off the Bookshelf
COLORING BOOK

45+ Weirdly Wonderful Designs to Color for Fun & Relaxation

Meet the Artist

Samarra Khaja makes happy, beautiful things inspired by her love of travel, local markets, food and culture, nostalgia, and her young sons. She revels in experimenting with the seemingly usual, turning it on its head and presenting it in a new unexpected light. She's also known for spending less time on her hair and more time on her drawing.

Living in New York City, she has worked across disciplines as a designer, photographer, art director, and illustrator for the likes of *The New York Times*, *The Guggenheim*, Bliss (spa and skin care), *Time* magazine, Victoria's Secret, and Cirque du Soleil—all in her signature whimsical style. She also designs textiles that mix contemporary design with a cheerful irreverence. They're bright, bold, and best of all, playful. Look for her fabric designs in shops worldwide and find fun projects to make in her new sewing project book, *Sew Adorkable*.

Learn more about Samarra at **samarrakhaja.com**.

C&T PUBLISHING ctpub.com   P.O. Box 1456 • Lafayette, CA 94549 • 800.284.1114   Copyright © 2015 by Samarra Khaja. All rights reserved.

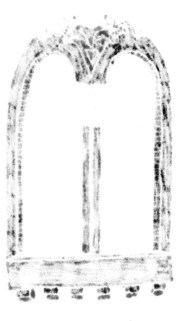

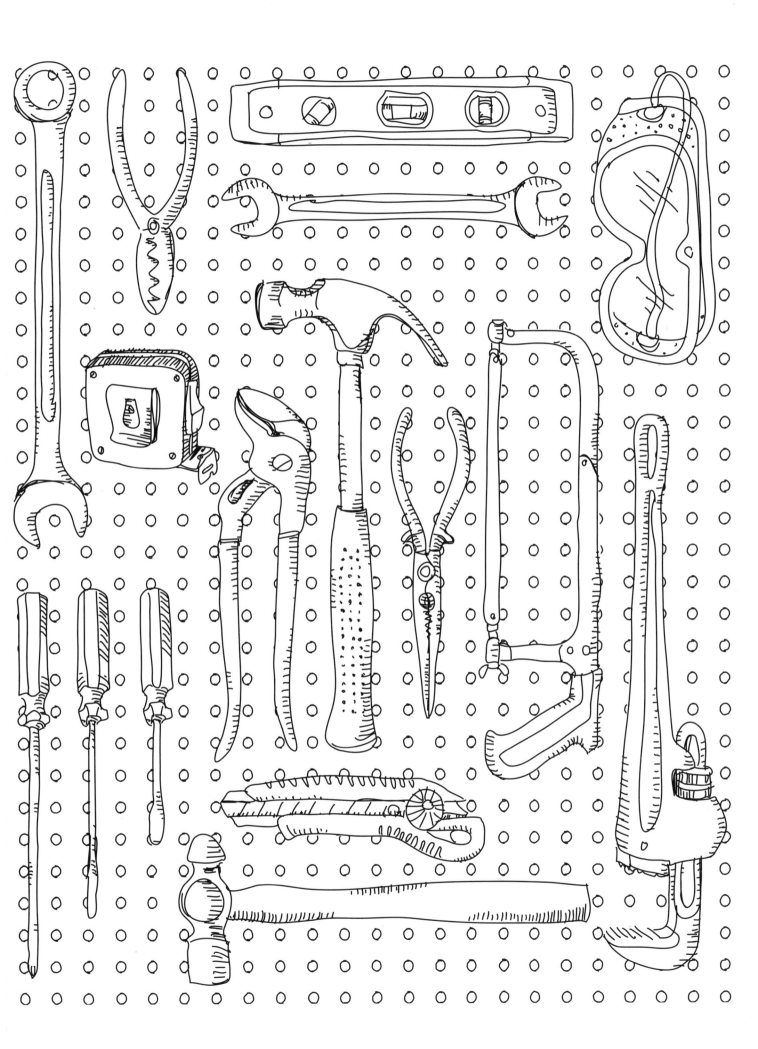

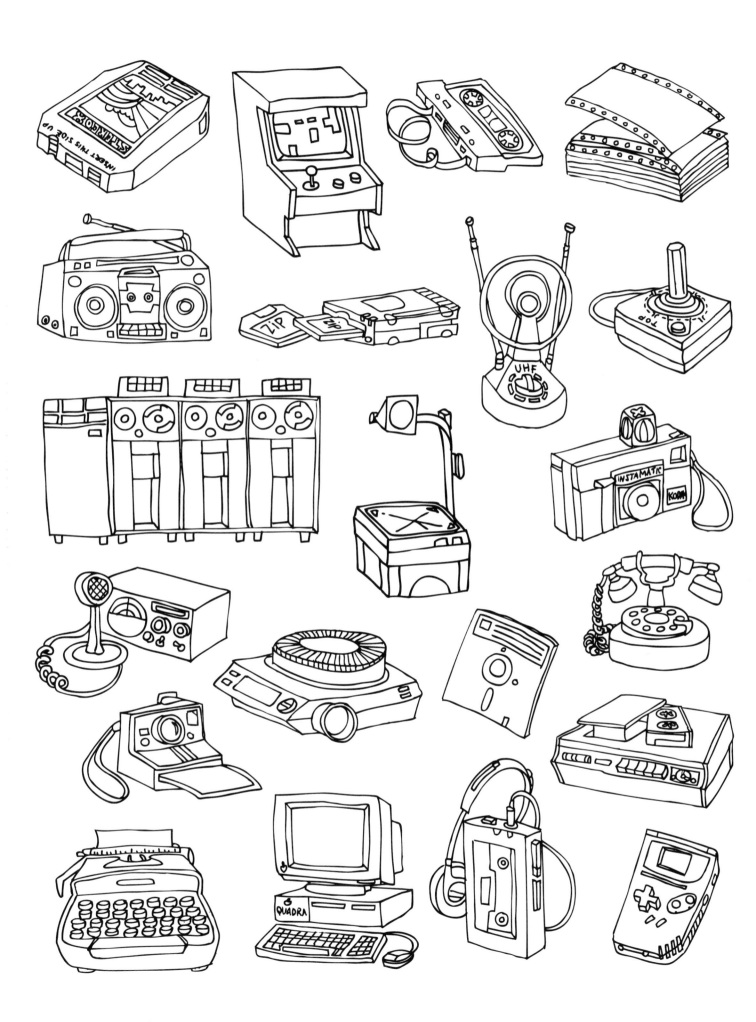

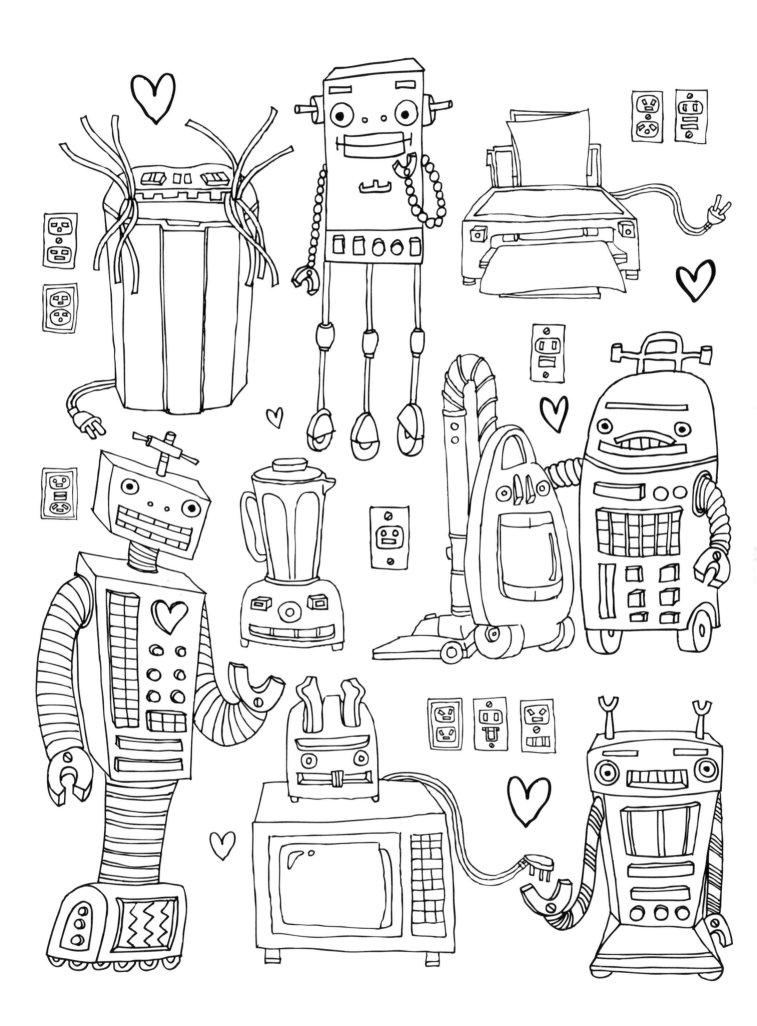

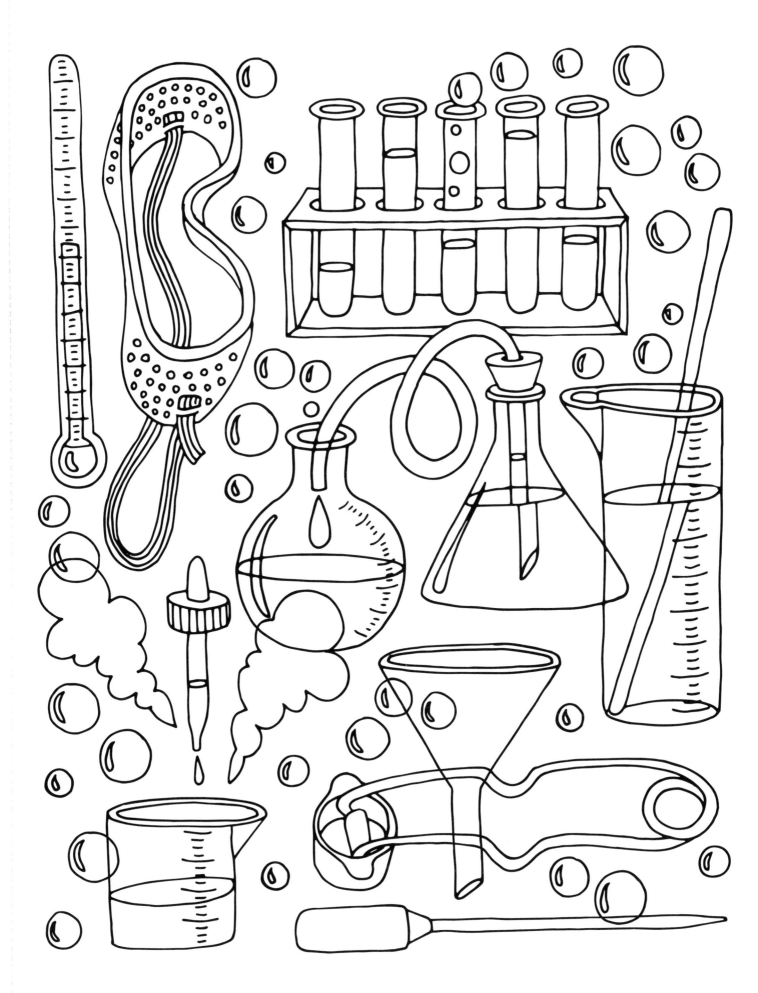